T0413657

BE RESPONSIBLE

by Sloane Hughes

Consultant: Beth Gambro
Reading Specialist, Yorkville, Illinois

BEARPORT
PUBLISHING

Minneapolis, Minnesota

Teaching Tips

Before Reading

- Look at the cover of the book. Discuss the picture and the title.

- Ask readers to brainstorm a list of what they already know about responsibility. What can they expect to see in this book?

- Go on a picture walk, looking through the pictures to discuss vocabulary and make predictions about the text.

During Reading

- Read for purpose. As they are reading, encourage readers to think about responsibility in their own lives.

- Ask readers to look for the details of the book. What are the specific ways someone can be responsible?

- If readers encounter an unknown word, ask them to look at the sounds in the word. Then, ask them to look at the rest of the page. Are there any clues to help them understand?

After Reading

- Encourage readers to pick a buddy and reread the book together.

- Ask readers to name two ways to be responsible that are included in the book. Go back and find the pages that tell about these things.

- Ask readers to write or draw something they learned about being responsible.

Credits:
Cover and title page, © Kraig Scarbinsky/iStock; 3, © annebaek/iStock; 5, © Monkey Business Images/Shutterstock; 6, © kool99/iStock; 8–9, © Kostikova Natalia/Shutterstock; 10–11, © SDI Productions/iStock; 13, © Studio Romantic/Shutterstock; 14, © Monkey Business Images/Shutterstock; 16, © djmilic/iStock; 17, © VioletaStoimenova/iStock; 18, © Chimpinski/iStock; 19, © JGA/Shutterstock; 20–21, © FatCamera/iStock; 22TL, © SerrNovik/iStock; 22TR, © New Africa/Shutterstock; 22BM, © SouthWorks/iStock; 23TL, © monkeybusinessimages/iStock; 23TR, © LightFieldStudios/iStock; 23BL, © SDI Productions/iStock; 23BM, © SDI Productions/iStock; and 23BR, © PeopleImages/iStock.

Library of Congress Cataloging-in-Publication Data

Names: Hughes, Sloane, author.
Title: Be responsible / by Sloane Hughes.
Description: Minneapolis, Minnesota : Bearport Publishing Company, [2023] |
Series: How awesome can you be? | Includes bibliographical references
and index.
Identifiers: LCCN 2022031848 (print) | LCCN 2022031849 (ebook) | ISBN
9798885093255 (library binding) | ISBN 9798885094474 (paperback) | ISBN
9798885095624 (ebook)
Subjects: LCSH: Responsibility--J uvenile literature.
Classification: LCC BJ1451 .H84 2023 (print) | LCC BJ1451 (ebook) | DDC
179/.9--dc23/eng/20220808
LC record available at https://lccn.loc.gov/2022031848
LC ebook record available at https://lccn.loc.gov/2022031849

For more information, write to Bearport Publishing, 5357 Penn Avenue South, Minneapolis, MN 55419.

Contents

Awesome to Be Responsible

Everybody has a job to do.

When we each do our part, it is better for everyone.

Being **responsible** is awesome!

5

Being responsible means taking care of your things.

You keep track of what is yours.

Being in charge of things is awesome!

How can you be responsible?

Put your toys away when you are done playing.

Everything has a place.

Return books to the library on time.

This means others can **enjoy** them, too.

That is being responsible with things that are not yours.

Sometimes, you may share spaces.

Picking up when you make a mess is responsible.

Then, you can enjoy a clean space with others!

13

People can count on you when you are responsible.

They **trust** you to do what you say you will.

Being responsible makes you a good friend.

You can be responsible by caring for others.

Help your brother learn something new.

Feeding pets is also responsible.

You are responsible when you can take care of yourself, too.

Eat well and **exercise**.

Brush your teeth every morning and night.

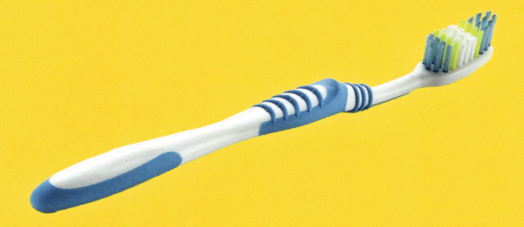

You can be awesome.

Being responsible is one way to do it.

Let's all do our part!

21

Showing Responsibility

Be responsible for your things at home.

1. Look around for things that are out of place.

2. Pick them up and put them away.

3. Help to clean the space. Then, it will be nice for everyone!

Glossary

enjoy to like a thing or doing something

exercise to move your body so you stay strong and healthy

responsible caring, trustworthy, and in charge

return to bring something back

trust to believe in someone or something

Index

Read More

Andrews, Elizabeth. *Understanding Responsibility (Understanding You).* Minneapolis: ABDO, 2023.

Krekelberg, Alyssa. *Doing the Right Thing: Making Responsible Decisions (Social and Emotional Learning).* Mankato, MN: The Child's World, 2021.

Learn More Online

1. Go to **www.factsurfer.com** or scan the QR code below.
2. Enter "**Be Responsible**" into the search box.
3. Click on the cover of this book to see a list of websites.

About the Author

Sloane Hughes is a writer living in New York. They have written many books for children and young adults.